W9-BNG-140

CAN YOUR

CONVERSATIONS

CHANGE THE WORLD?

BOOK SOLD
NO LONGER R.H.P.L.
PROPERTY

a popactivism book

CAN YOUR
CONVERSATIONS
CHANGE THE WORLD?

Erinne Paisley

ORCA BOOK PUBLISHERS

Text copyright © 2018 Erinne Paisley

All rights reserved. No part of this publication may be reproduced or transmitted in any form or by any means, electronic or mechanical, including photocopying, recording or by any information storage and retrieval system now known or to be invented, without permission in writing from the publisher.

Cataloguing in Publication information available from Library and Archives Canada

Issued in print and electronic formats.
ISBN 978-1-4598-1309-0 (softcover).—ISBN 978-1-4598-1310-6 (pdf).—ISBN 978-1-4598-1311-3 (epub)

First published in the United States, 2018
Library of Congress Control Number: 2018933718

Summary: This work of nonfiction in the PopActivism series for teens looks at the importance of talking about feminism and continuing to fight for equal rights.

Orca Book Publishers is dedicated to preserving the environment and has printed this book on Forest Stewardship Council® certified paper.

Orca Book Publishers gratefully acknowledges the support for its publishing programs provided by the following agencies: the Government of Canada through the Canada Book Fund and the Canada Council for the Arts, and the Province of British Columbia through the BC Arts Council and the Book Publishing Tax Credit.

The author and publisher have made every effort to ensure that the information in this book was correct at the time of publication. The author and publisher do not assume any liability for any loss, damage or disruption caused by errors or omissions. Every effort has been made to trace copyright holders and to obtain their permission for the use of copyrighted material. The publisher apologizes for any errors or omissions and would be grateful if notified of any corrections that should be incorporated in future reprints or editions of this book.

Edited by Sarah N. Harvey
Design by Jenn Playford
Cover and flap images by Ute Muller/fotoartphotography.net
Thank you to Feminist Apparel for providing Erinne with her #FEMINIST T-shirt.
Author photo by Jacklyn Atlas

ORCA BOOK PUBLISHERS
orcabook.com

Printed and bound in Canada.

RICHMOND HILL PUBLIC LIBRARY
3297 2001085291   RH
Can your conversation change the world?
Sep. 10, 2018

To Alana Charlton
and Erin Hayes

CONTENTS

ACTIVISM

The creation of social and/or
political change.

POP**ACTIVISM**

Activism fused with pop culture.

pop**activism**

see change. share change. be change

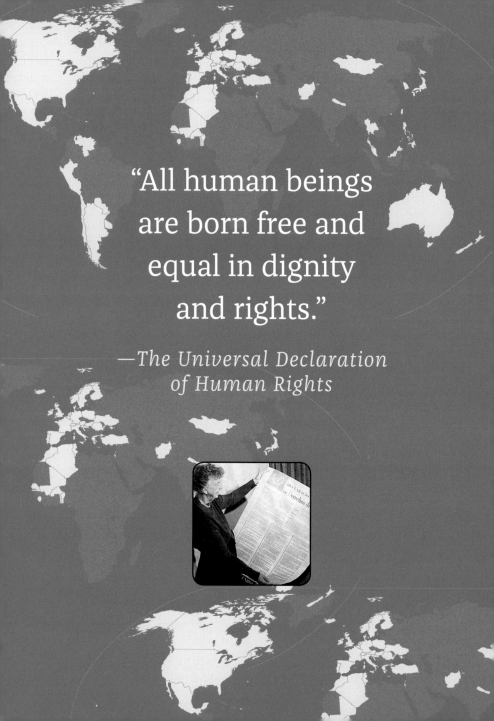

"All human beings
are born free and
equal in dignity
and rights."

—*The Universal Declaration
of Human Rights*

1

A DIFFERENT TYPE OF EDUCATION

WHEN I WAS YOUNG MY PARENTS TAUGHT ME a lot about human rights. There are even old pictures of me in my living room with Amnesty International posters in the background. Amnesty International fights all over the world for everyone to have their basic human rights fulfilled no matter their age, gender, nationality, ethnicity or religion. These rights are laid out in detail in the Universal Declaration of Human Rights, which was adopted by the United Nations General Assembly in 1948.

As I got older I learned about the many human rights violations that occur all over the world every day. For example, some people do not have access to clean drinking water. Others are forced into marriage before they are adults. Denial of human rights also often takes the form of physical harm, such as torture or rape. I started to realize that one group of people in particular seemed to suffer from a lot of human rights violations across the globe—women.

This was shocking to me, because I am female! Sure, I have been called "bossy," and I realized long ago that girls and women are often expected to act a certain way. But I have never experienced any significant discrimination. And yet all over the world, women are facing human rights violations simply because they are female!

When we had self-directed studies in my middle school, I decided to study human rights violations and women's rights. I learned that less than a third of adolescent girls in sub-Saharan Africa and less than half of adolescent girls in South Asia are enrolled in secondary school. Around two-thirds of illiterate adults are women. Globally, a girl under the age of fifteen gets married every seven seconds. *Every seven seconds.*

I wanted to be able to help, but I didn't really know how. When I got to high school I began to realize that women's rights issues also affected me. People had fought in the past for a woman's right to vote and to control her own body, and for pay equity. But the fight is far from over. Women still make far less than men do while doing the same jobs. Women are still expected to look and act a certain way, and we are still told what we can do with our bodies. As well, according to a national study in the United States, one in four women in college report having survived rape or attempted rape. Facts like these made me aware that the battle for women's rights still needs to be fought all over the world.

GLOBALLY, A GIRL UNDER THE AGE OF FIFTEEN GETS MARRIED EVERY SEVEN SECONDS.

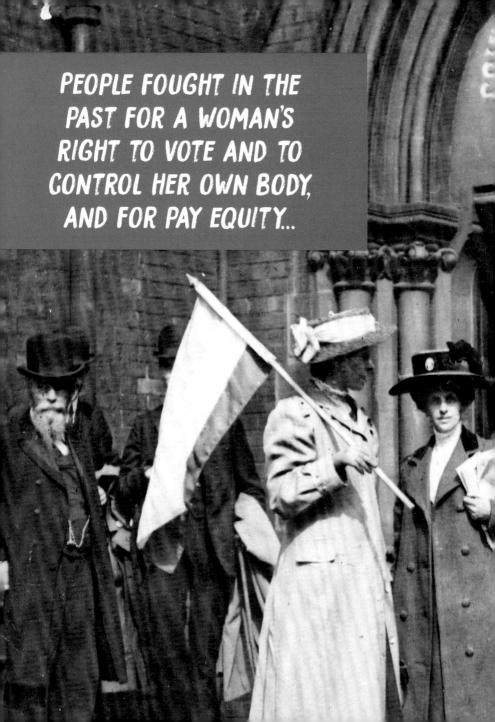

PEOPLE FOUGHT IN THE PAST FOR A WOMAN'S RIGHT TO VOTE AND TO CONTROL HER OWN BODY, AND FOR PAY EQUITY...

British suffragists demonstrating for the right to vote in 1911.
JOHNNY CYPRUS

My friend Preet Walia poses during the Women's March in Toronto, ON, January 2017. ERINNE PAISLEY

A picture of change

...BUT THE FIGHT IS FAR FROM OVER.

By the end of high school, I knew that the fight for women's rights deals with media images of an ideal body, the lack of educational opportunities for girls around the world, the intersection of race, class and gender, and many other issues. I'd also learned about the power that comes when women's rights are upheld. For instance, educating girls has been shown to largely improve economies, which means girls' education can literally end poverty.

That is when I definitely knew I was a feminist.

When I graduated from high school in 2015, I thought it made sense to use some of the exciting and celebratory energy around graduation to try and bring extra awareness to the issue of women's educational rights. I created my prom dress out of paper instead

EDUCATING GIRLS HAS BEEN SHOWN TO LARGELY IMPROVE ECONOMIES, WHICH MEANS GIRLS' EDUCATION CAN LITERALLY END POVERTY.

of buying a dress, and I wrote on it in red ink *I've received my education. Not every woman has that right. Malala.org.* I donated the money I would have spent on a grad dress to the Malala Fund. Every time someone asked about my grad dress, I encouraged them to visit Malala.org to learn more about the fight for women's rights worldwide and donate what they could! I hoped that the money raised would be able to help even just one other girl get the education I had taken for granted.

Then something amazing happened—the story went viral. You can read more about that story in *Can Your Smartphone Change the World?* and *Can Your Outfit Change the World?* The story was shared many, many times, but the reactions came in many different shapes and forms. Most people loved the idea of helping women receive an education and have equal opportunities. But other people did not like it. Some people wrote nasty comments and even threatened me, saying I didn't belong in the classroom, that I was being too loud, that women don't deserve equal opportunities and that it was not my place to speak out about other people's rights.

My dress was made out of my Pre-Calculus 11 homework. I wrote on it with red pen to match the corrections that were still on it.
UTE MULLER/
FOTOARTPHOTOGRAPHY.NET

HOW CAN YOU HELP CREATE MORE EQUAL OPPORTUNITIES FOR EVERYONE? AND WHY DO WE STILL NEED TO FIGHT THESE BATTLES IN 2018? AREN'T THE MAIN FEMINIST BATTLES ALREADY WON?

It was scary and shocking, and it highlighted once again the work that still has to be done!

When the story of my prom dress for women's education went viral, many of the places that shared the story originally were feminist online communities. They featured stories of female *empowerment,* amplified strong female voices and continued the fight for a more equal world! I started to read more of these blogs and connect with more people all over the world who identify as feminists. What does gender equality mean? What women's rights still need to be put in place around the world? How can you help create more equal opportunities for everyone? And why do we still need to fight these battles in 2018? Aren't the main feminist battles already won?

Many books and articles have been written about feminism. People all over the world study feminism. They are speaking out, learning, teaching, and having conversations. I do not have a degree in gender studies. As I write this book, I am still a teenager, and I am still learning as I go. But one thing I do know is that if we want to create a more equal world, we need to have more conversations about what equality looks like, how it can be possible and how we can measure its progress. We need to have conversations with those who agree with us *and* with those who do not. The more conversations we have, the more change can happen. My hope for this book is that it creates a conversation—between you and me, between us and the world.

Get together with your friends and start conversations that matter. CREATISTA/SHUTTERSTOCK.COM

"Holding back women is holding back half of every country in the world."

—Amal Clooney

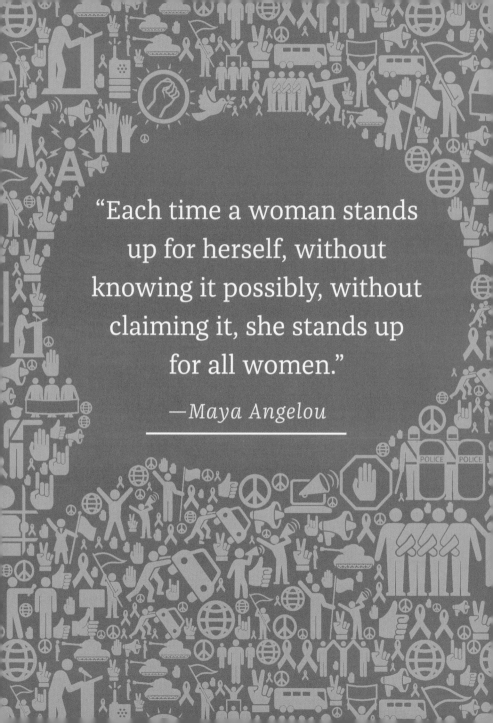

"Each time a woman stands up for herself, without knowing it possibly, without claiming it, she stands up for all women."

—*Maya Angelou*

2

THE F WORD

WHAT DOES FEMINISM ACTUALLY MEAN?
According to the Merriam-Webster dictionary the word *feminist* means someone who believes in "the political, economic and social equality of the sexes." In other words, a feminist believes that people are equal to one another no matter their sex. Being a feminist can mean different things to different people, but it always includes the belief in equality and human rights.

Millicent Fawcett (third from left, bottom row), the founder of the National Union of Women's Suffrage Societies, sits with other women leaders at the Suffrage Alliance Congress in London, England, in 1909.

NASJONALBIBLIOTEKET/WIKIPEDIA.ORG

THE FIRST WAVE

The history of feminism is loosely organized into a number of periods when women have fought for specific rights. These periods are often called the "waves of feminism." The first wave was from the 1830s to the 1900s. Feminists around the world protested, demanding more political and legal rights for women, including the right to vote, which they had always been denied. In England during this time, the National Union of Women's Suffrage Societies was founded by Millicent Fawcett. *Suffrage* means the right to vote. Some women called themselves *suffragists* and protested for the right to vote. In 1893 the British colony of New Zealand granted women the right to vote. By 1920 most women were finally allowed to vote in the United States; in Canada, some women had the vote in 1918, but it wasn't until 1940 that all white women in Canada could vote. It was only in 1960 that Indigenous people were allowed to vote. Japanese Canadians could not vote till 1948. None of this could have happened if women (and their allies) hadn't spoken up and demanded their basic human rights. A lot has happened in a hundred years, but there's still more to do.

THE SECOND WAVE

Between the 1960s and the 1980s the second wave of feminism continued the fight. Women had become more equal in some ways—they could vote and they could own property—but they were still not truly equal. For example, in Canada in 1960 women were paid less then men in almost every field—around

Women hold up signs saying *Women Demand Equality* and *I'm a Second Class Citizen* at a women's liberation march in Washington, DC, 1970.
U.S. NEWS & WORLD REPORT, LIBRARY OF CONGRESS/WIKIPEDIA.ORG

sixty-one cents an hour to do the same job a man would get paid one dollar an hour to do. Women also did not have a lot of rights over their own bodies. They could not get easy access to *contraception* (ways to prevent pregnancy), and it was illegal in most countries to get an *abortion* (end a pregnancy). Many people still believed that women were created to be "barefoot, pregnant and in the kitchen." They were not seen as equal members of society deserving of equal opportunities. Women and their allies held protests and engaged in public

displays of rebellion (such as throwing their restrictive bras and girdles in the garbage). They formed consciousness-raising groups so they could talk freely about their lives as women. They demanded a change in the way society looked at and valued women, but it was an uphill battle.

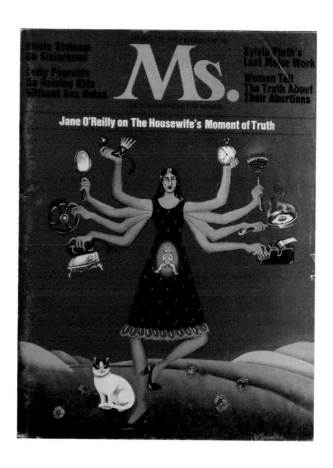

Feminist Movie Night

Every day we continue to learn about the world around us, and the more we learn about something, the more we become able to change it! One fun way to learn more about feminism is through movies such as *Miss Representation*, *She's Beautiful When She's Angry*, *Girl Rising* and *Dream, Girl*. They can all start more discussions about feminism. Check out online lists of feminist movies for other ideas.

By hosting a Feminist Movie Night, you can start a conversation in your school or with your friends about what feminism is and how you can fight for gender equality. If you organize it through your school, you can even charge a small fee for tickets and donate the money to a charity of your choice. Have a guided discussion after the movie to talk about what you learned and how we can work together to create a more equal world!

"A feminist is anyone who recognizes the equality and full humanity of women and men."

—*Gloria Steinem*

POP QUIZ

How can you be an *ally*?

An ally is someone who supports a cause that doesn't necessarily affect them directly. To be an effective ally, it's important to start by learning more. What do you know about these issues? Who can you ask and what can you read to learn more? How can you support those who are impacted by these differences?

THE THIRD WAVE

The third wave of feminism began in the 1990s and continues to the present. Feminists are still fighting for many of the things that people began fighting for in the 1960s, but there is even more focus on *intersectionality* (covered in the next section), on ending violence toward women (a topic that has often been pushed under the rug and not talked about publically) and on expanding the boundaries of gender awareness (this includes talking about sexuality and gender on a spectrum).

Some people have suggested there is a fourth wave of feminism, which began around 2009. This wave is said to focus on online communities of feminists. The term is credited to Jessica Valenti, founder of *Feministing,* an online community for young feminists.

FEMINISTS ARE STILL FIGHTING FOR MANY OF THE THINGS THAT PEOPLE BEGAN FIGHTING FOR IN THE 1960S.

INTERSECTIONALITY

Intersectional feminism recognizes how complex people's lives are and how inequality affects each person differently. We are not all simply one thing, physically or culturally. It's important to acknowledge that factors like race, gender, sexual orientation, class, ability and ethnicity play a big part in how people experience inequality. Intersectional feminism acknowledges how these intersections might make one person's experience of sexism and inequality different from another's.

Rowan Blanchard, the star of *Girl Meets World*, runs her own online blog through Tumblr. When she was fourteen she wrote an essay response to a question sent to her Tumblr about what feminism really means to her.

FACTORS LIKE RACE, GENDER, SEXUAL ORIENTATION, CLASS, ABILITY AND ETHNICITY PLAY A BIG PART IN HOW PEOPLE EXPERIENCE INEQUALITY.

Protesters march under an LGBTQ rainbow flag in Sao Paulo, Brazil, on May 28, 2016. These activists were marching for the rights of gay women and the end of the *coup d'état* in their country.
FERNANDOPODOLSKI/SHUTTERSTOCK.COM

Rowan focused on starting a discussion on intersectional feminism when she said in the essay, *The way a black woman experiences sexism and inequality is different from the way a white woman experiences sexism and inequality. Likewise with trans women and Hispanic women. While white women are making 78 cents to the dollar, Native American women are making 65 cents, black women are making 64 cents, and Hispanic women are making 54 cents.*

Rowan Blanchard's post about intersectional feminism got over five thousand notes on Tumblr and became part of a discussion about what modern feminism means. Rowan continues to write about her own experiences as a young feminist and all she is learning as she continues to explore what feminism can be. In December 2016 she and one of her best friends, Yara Shahidi, guest-edited and posed on the cover of the *Teen Vogue* activist issue. Rowan spoke again about the importance of embracing intersectional feminism: *Like [activist] DeRay McKesson says, "You're not born woke"; it's such a learning process. I started thinking about the feminism I was initially being sold, which was basically that boys and girls should be equal. But there are intersections, and a lot of reasons why it is easier for me to achieve that equality than it is for some of my friends. You have to always question your politics: Am I being as inclusive as I possibly can?*

"You have to always question your politics: Am I being as inclusive as I possibly can?"

—Rowan Blanchard

HeForShe

Who is allowed to be a feminist? The answer is easy—everyone! Not just women. Some people still believe that only individuals who identify as female can be feminists. Emma Watson started the HeForShe campaign with the United Nations to show that anyone can be a feminist and that it's important for lots of different types of people to call themselves feminists. The campaign's goal is to get more men and boys involved as "agents of change" fighting for gender equality and women's rights. Emma gave a speech at the United Nations to start the campaign, and the speech was uploaded to YouTube, where it has had nearly two million views!

HeForShe invites anyone to use the hashtag #HeForShe to join the campaign. Joining means signing the HeForShe commitment, which says "I am one of billions who believe that everyone is born free and equal. I will take action against *gender bias*, discrimination and violence to bring the benefits of equality to us all." The HeForShe campaign wants to start more conversations about gender equality—and you can join the conversation through its hashtag or by visiting heforshe.org. As of 2016, 1.3 billion conversations have been started on social media by using this hashtag!

HeForShe

UN Women Solidarity Movement
for Gender Equality

GLOBAL FEMINISM

Women all over the world still live without the privileges that we in developed countries take for granted, like the right to vote and the right to a free education. According to UN Women, more than 700 million women alive right now have been forced against their will into marriage before the age of eighteen. UN Women is a "global champion for gender quality" and part of the United Nations.

NOT ALLOWING WOMEN TO VOTE SAYS THAT WOMEN AND MEN ARE NOT EQUAL IN THE EYES OF THE LAW.

In Vatican City, where the Pope lives, women still are not allowed to vote, and in Saudi Arabia women only became eligible to vote for the first time in municipal elections in 2015. Not allowing women to vote says that women and men are not equal in the eyes of the law. In Yemen, women are not allowed by law to leave the house without their husbands' permission. In many places around the world (including

A number of male feminists showed their support for equal rights at the Women's March in Toronto, January 2017. **ERINNE PAISLEY**

in North America), when a woman is raped (sexual interaction that is *nonconsensual)* the woman, not the attacker, is often blamed for the assault. Some people believe that women "ask" to be assaulted when they wear "provocative" clothing or are in the "wrong" place. None of this is true, because rape is never ever the fault of the survivor.

Being a feminist clearly means a lot of different things. *Sexism*—prejudice, stereotyping and discrimination against people based on their sex—affects everyone differently. Learning what being a feminist means and figuring out how you can help fight for gender equality should be an ongoing conversation for everyone. Education is power, and discussion is always the first step to creating meaningful change.

EDUCATION IS POWER, AND DISCUSSION IS ALWAYS THE FIRST STEP TO CREATING MEANINGFUL CHANGE.

The United Nations headquarters are located in Manhattan, NY.
ERINNE PAISLEY

UN WOMEN IS A "GLOBAL CHAMPION FOR GENDER QUALITY" AND PART OF THE UNITED NATIONS.

"Hashtags, shares, likes
and comments let you
hold activist power in the
palm of your hand."

—*Erinne Paisley*

3

HASHTAG EQUALITY

MY FIRST BOOK, *CAN YOUR SMARTPHONE CHANGE THE WORLD?*, was about how social media can create opportunities for change. Social media allows us to connect with more people, ideas and realities than ever before. These tools can be used to start discussions, change what our world considers "normal" or acceptable, and organize positive world change. Hashtags, shares, likes and comments let you hold activist power in the palm of your hand.

#COOL2CARE

When I was in twelfth grade I was curious about what other people thought feminism meant and how they thought we could help create more equality worldwide. I got a few of my friends to help me organize a pizza party at lunchtime in a spare classroom and invited everyone at the school to come and discuss feminism. Around thirty people turned up—I mean, who can turn down free pizza? We heard from a guest speaker, a master's student at our local university who had fought for women's rights in Serbia and was now studying leadership. We then went around the circle, sharing our thoughts on what feminism means and how we can create change. The longer we talked, the more people shared. Some people even got into debates and challenged each other's points of view. This is how change begins!

THE LONGER WE TALKED, THE MORE PEOPLE SHARED. THIS IS HOW CHANGE BEGINS!

Using social media to start in-person discussions allowed us to address points of view that were different from our own and have more meaningful conversations that were not just in a comments section. Social media can be very helpful in organizing more meaningful IRL discussions such as this one. In person, it's easier to read someone's body language and talk in a more compassionate way about topics that can often be sensitive and emotionally charged.

We decided we wanted to do something as a group to create a more equal and accepting world, starting in a small way. We agreed that in our high school it wasn't considered cool to care about feminism, especially if you were male. We wanted to change this. So we created a PSA, or *public service announcement*, on why it's #cool2care. In the video, which we posted on YouTube, a few older boys talked about why they believe it's cool to care about feminism. Then we showed the video at a school assembly and encouraged everyone to share on social media why they believe it's #cool2care!

POP QUIZ

How do you deal with online hate?

One issue that arises when starting conversations online is hate. It's easy to hide behind a keyboard and vent your aggression by making mean comments online. Topics such as feminism almost always arouse lots of emotions—both positive and negative. Online this often translates to "comment wars" or dislikes. How do you deal with this online hate and still have meaningful conversations?

On some social media platforms, such as Instagram, you can actually go into the app and prevent certain words from being posted in your comments. These can be very hurtful words that you don't want to be present on your account. If it is someone you know commenting, it's always more productive to have a private conversation with that person—this can be through private messaging or in person, if you feel safe with this person. This is an ongoing issue with social media, and one that is continuing to be studied and worked on.

The most important thing is to remember that you are talking to another human being. Without compassion, conversations can very easily lead to disagreements instead of progress.

BOYS WHO LOVE PINK

Advertising, TV shows, movies and celebrity culture tell boys how to be men, often by sending the message that it's not okay to express themselves in what's seen as a feminine way. This is negative not only because it devalues women, but also because it limits self-expression. Boys are told that it's not "manly" to show emotion, that they need to be aggressive and look physically strong, or that they are not "masculine" if they like things that are almost exclusively marketed to girls. The idea that boys need to "man up" instead of expressing themselves in a healthy and peaceful way is called *hypermasculinity*, and it is harmful to both men and women.

In 2014 Martine Zoer created the online campaign #freetowearpink. She also designed a line of pink clothing called Quirkie Kids for both girls and boys in response to hearing about a boy being teased for wearing pink to school. She wrote, *No kid should be teased for what they wear! Some boys like pink and why not? Pink is just a color and so is green, and blue, and yellow.* People were invited to use the hashtag

French rugby player Jules Plisson and his teammates often wear pink.
MARIE-LAN NGUYEN/WIKIPEDIA.ORG

#freetowearpink when they posted pictures of themselves or their children wearing pink. This sends the message that there's no one way to be manly or masculine, just as there's no one way to be feminine.

#GROWINGUPAGIRL

In 2015 a hashtag campaign called #GrowingUpAGirl started trending on social media. The hashtag brought awareness to some of the ways sexism can negatively affect both boys and girls as they grow up. One Twitter user tweeted, *#GrowingUpAGirl being told I have to take down a picture cause people are going to look at me the wrong way.* Another popular tweet read *#GrowingUpAGirl being taught from a young age that my body is a distraction to boys rather than a vessel through which to live my life.* I joined the Twitter conversation by tweeting a few posts, including *#GrowingUpAGirl being called "bossy" instead of "having leadership potential" when you do anything beyond sitting & listening.*

Many people retweeted and joined the campaign, helping to show how relatable and real these experiences were. Joining a hashtag campaign through social media can help you connect with like-minded people, show support and learn something new. You can even start your own hashtag campaign; you never know—it might start trending!

The Strand is a famous bookstore in New York City that contains lots of books and products that focus on activism. This bag is from Strand Bookstore and features a literary version of the We Can Do It! image. ERINNE PAISLEY

Riley's Rant

What else do advertising and marketing tell us about gender roles? Have you ever noticed that lots of toys are designed to be for either boys or girls? A seven-year-old girl named Riley noticed, and she didn't understand why this was happening, since she believed anyone should be able to play with any type of toy. Her dad took a video of Riley in a toy store and it went viral. She pretty much sums up gender bias when she says, "It wouldn't be fair for all the girls to buy princesses and for all the boys to buy superheroes. Because girls want superheroes and the boys want superheroes, and the girls want pink stuff and the boys want pink stuff." Next time you go shopping, remember what Riley said, and question gender bias in marketing. You can email companies and ask why they are marketing their products this way and ask them to change their ways! You can usually find a company's email on its online homepage. You can also start a conversation by asking people who work at your favorite stores why they sort their products by gender.

POSITIVE CHANGE ONLINE

There are many communities online that support equality, amplify women's voices, fight for human rights and share some funny stories along the way. These online feminist communities have taught me a lot about gender equality and the need for action. Some of these communities shared the story of my paper grad dress for women's education, allowing me to connect with people all over the world who also want to create positive change. Your smartphone is a tool for activism and creating change. It can

YOUR SMARTPHONE IS A TOOL FOR ACTIVISM AND CREATING CHANGE.

be used to learn, connect with others and create a more equal world. If you have a social media account or smartphone, you can start exploring new ways to be #woke with a few clicks on your screen. These are some of my favorite feminist online communities.

WOMENYOUSHOULDKNOW.NET

Women You Should Know features stories about women who deserve recognition and news headlines, but who all too often don't get either. Jennifer Jones and Cynthia Hornig started *Women You Should Know* to create a connected and supportive community that celebrates women's accomplishments.

LENNYLETTER.COM

Lenny Letter is a website and online newsletter created by actress and writer Lena Dunham and writer and director Jenni Konner. Through *Lenny Letter* they amplify voices, stories and discussions on feminism, style, politics, friendship, work and much more!

Jenni Konner (left) and Lena Dunham, the founders of LennyLetter.com.
KATHY HUTCHINS/SHUTTERSTOCK.COM

MY FAVORITE F WORD IS FEMINISM

My Favorite F Word Is Feminism is a Facebook page created by *Bustle*, an online feminist magazine. It shares feminist stories from all over the Internet so you can read, share, comment and like them!

AMYSMARTGIRLS.COM

Amy Poehler's *Smart Girls* is a website and social media entity founded by—you guessed it—actress and activist Amy Poehler. It strives to help young people in particular create and stay true to their authentic selves. The website says, *We emphasize intelligence and imagination over "fitting in." We celebrate curiosity over gossip. We are a place people can truly be their weird and wonderful selves.*

Left to right: Mindy Kaling, Amy Poehler and Phyllis Smith.
FEATUREFLASH PHOTO AGENCY/SHUTTERSTOCK.COM

ROOKIEMAG.COM

Rookie is an online publication and print magazine that features written work and illustrations by teenage creators. Tavi Gevinson, the editor-in-chief, says she founded *Rookie* when she was a teenager because she didn't feel like there were enough voices she could actually relate to in the media around her. Today the website and publication have a large following and have started conversations by and for teens for over seven years.

Tavi Gevinson, founder of *Rookie Mag*, speaks with Janet Mock, author and trans-rights activist, at the launch of Janet's 2017 book *Surpassing Certainty.*
ERINNE PAISLEY

I got the chance to attend Janet Mock's book launch at the Strand Bookstore in New York City, where I spoke with Tavi about social media activism. ERINNE PAISLEY

On September 12, 1992, Mae Jemison became the first African American woman to travel in space when she went into orbit aboard the Space Shuttle *Endeavour*.
NASA/WIKIPEDIA.ORG

Charlotte Cooper became the first female Olympic tennis champion as well as the first individual female Olympic champion in Paris on July 11, 1900.
OLYMPICS.ORG/WIKIPEDIA.ORG

Grace Hopper was a pioneer of computer programming. On November 22, 2016, she was posthumously awarded the Presidential Medal of Freedom by then president Barack Obama. LYNN GILBERT/WIKIPEDIA.ORG

"The right way is not always the popular and easy way. Standing for right when it is unpopular is a true test of moral character."

—*Margaret Chase Smith*

Margaret Chase Smith (right) was the first woman to serve in both houses of the United States Congress. First Lady Eleanor Roosevelt (left) advocated for expanded roles for women in the workplace, the civil rights of African Americans and Asian Americans, and the rights of World War II refugees. In 1956, Chase and Roosevelt were the first-ever women panelists on *Face the Nation*, one of the longest-running news programs in television history. **US NATIONAL ARCHIVES/WIKIPEDIA.ORG**

"No woman can call herself
free who does not own and
control her body."

—Margaret Sanger

4

YOUR BODY, YOUR CHOICE

POPULAR CULTURE IS DEFINED as cultural activities or commercial products aimed at the tastes of the mainstream population—particularly young people. Pop culture is reflected in advertising, television, movies, fashion, music and video games. It has a lot of power, especially when it comes to how we think about our bodies. According to popular culture there is a "right" way to look and act. There is a lot of *body shaming* online, ridiculing specific body types even if they are healthy.

Popular culture also exists offline, putting pressure on women to *not* do certain things with their bodies—such as have abortions. In reality, the only person who has the right to comment on or decide what you do with your body is you!

THE RIGHT TO CHOOSE

"My body, my choice!" is a chant that is often associated with protests supporting women's reproductive rights. Abortions are performed when a woman chooses to terminate a pregnancy before a baby is fully formed (usually before twelve weeks). An abortion, when done correctly, is a safe medical procedure. There are many reasons why someone might choose to get an abortion. For instance, she may have become pregnant through rape. She may not feel ready to have a child or cannot afford to raise one. In many places abortion is still illegal, and women are forced to use dangerous, sometimes life-threatening methods to end their pregnancies.

PLANNED PARENTHOOD

Planned Parenthood is an organization that has been working for over one hundred years to support women when they are considering having an abortion. It also provides education and resources on other reproductive health topics, such as contraception. It wants to "give women the knowledge to control birth." Planned Parenthood was founded on the idea that women should be able to have the information and resources they need to "live strong, healthy lives and fulfill their dreams." Planned Parenthood believes the only person who should make the decision about what is right and wrong for a woman is the woman herself!

You can learn more about the fight for female reproductive health at plannedparenthood.org. You can also watch a short animated film made about the organization by NowThis News called *The History of 100 Years of Women's Health Care at Planned Parenthood* to learn more.

All over the world, women's voices are being heard. Clockwise from top left: COAST-TO-COAST/ISTOCK.COM, RENA SCHILD / SHUTTERSTOCK.COM, JONATAN SVENSSON GLAD/ WIKIPEDIA.ORG, A KATZ/SHUTTERSTOCK.COM.

Consent

What is consent? Consent is agreeing to, giving permission for or saying "yes" to sexual activity with another person or persons. If the other person says no, their wishes must be respected. No means no, and yes must be said clearly and enthusiastically to mean yes. If drugs or alcohol are involved, it is even more important to check in with a sexual partner. Sex without consent is assault, and it is illegal. Asking for consent from another person shows respect and indicates that you are checking in with that person. You always have to make sure that all people are comfortable when engaging in sexual activity.

PHOTOSHOP EVOLUTION

In *Can Your Outfit Change the World?* I wrote about how important it is to try to dissect popular culture in order to better understand its influence on your life. If you question it, you can start to change the negative messages that are out there.

Many images you see today are altered to conform to a specific body type. Pimples are erased and waistlines are curved inward. It's pretty clear that today's "ideal body" often isn't even physically possible. One of the first viral videos about photoshopping was Dove's 2007 *Evolution* video, which shows what happens from photo shoot to final photo. Hours of hair and makeup are fast-forwarded, the photos are taken, and then Photoshop or another image-editing software is used to change the shape of the woman's

IT'S PRETTY CLEAR THAT TODAY'S "IDEAL BODY" OFTEN ISN'T EVEN PHYSICALLY POSSIBLE.

POP QUIZ

What are your favorite magazines or television programs telling you about beauty?

Can you tell if some of the pictures are photoshopped? You can write directly to many magazines by visiting their website and finding their email address in the About section. Some magazines even allow you to write letters to the editor, which might be published in the magazine. You can ask them to stop using image-editing software so much and increase body positivity through more realistic images!

face, the length of her neck, etc. At the end the video states, *No wonder our perception of beauty is distorted.*

Since its release, millions of people have viewed the video. It has been used to teach about body image in schools. A study done in 2011 claimed that just watching the *Evolution* video increased people's confidence in their own bodies because they understood the process created something that wasn't "normal" or "real." The video was also a part of Dove's larger Self-Esteem Project. This project has been used to teach body confidence and empowerment to women instead of selling them products by promoting unrealistic beauty standards.

Some scholars have questioned Dove's approach to creating these videos because they still send the message that validation and happiness come from physical beauty. But Dove's *Evolution* video did create a lot of awareness about the extent to which image-editing software and professional hair and makeup alter the images we see every day.

LEARNING ABOUT OUR BODIES

I remember getting "the talk" in middle school. Everyone had a different idea of what "the talk" would include, and kids whispered about it in the halls in the days leading up to it. The rumors were put to rest when we learned that "the talk" was about the basics of sex and contraception. What I remember most about it was being separated from the boys to be given a "gift." I was superexcited, assuming it was going to be chocolate or something equally delicious. I was fairly disappointed when I discovered it was not a snack—it was a sanitary pad for when our periods started.

WHAT I REMEMBER MOST ABOUT IT WAS BEING SEPARATED FROM THE BOYS TO BE GIVEN A "GIFT."

In most schools "the talk" does not answer all the questions one might have about sex and sexuality. For Laci Green this was definitely the case. Growing up, Laci had a lot of unanswered questions

POP QUIZ

What does your school's version of "the talk" include?

Does it discuss consent or educate on sexuality or gender? If not, is there a safe space to ask questions about these topics? Talk to your principal or school counselor about including important topics like consent in course curricula. You could even start a petition to make sure that consent is taught in schools and included in all discussions about sex.

SKEPTICAL FEMINISM MEANS THAT YOU KEEP QUESTIONING THE WAY THINGS ARE, EVEN THINGS THAT ARE NOT USUALLY QUESTIONED.

about sex and sexuality. She wanted to be able to decide what to do with her own body and be better educated about these topics. After university she became a sex educator and started a YouTube channel called *Sex+* to educate and empower people about their own bodies. This begins with learning about all the options, and Laci tries to make this information easy to access and talk about!

Laci was nineteen when she started her YouTube channel in 2008, and it now has over 1.5million subscribers and viewers worldwide. She also has an online blog and uses Twitter, Tumblr, Facebook and Snapchat. She says that when she first started her channel she wanted to "help young people who, like me, had been told that their sexuality was bad or wrong and that they were less because of their gender or sexual orientation." Some of her videos talk about how gender is on a spectrum. Others talk about consent and how you must have your partner's explicit permission to engage in any sexual activity for it to be consensual.

Laci Green calls herself an intersectional, sex-positive and skeptical feminist. You read about intersectional feminism in Chapter 2. Sex-positive feminism views sex as a positive thing as long as it is healthy and consensual. Skeptical feminism means that you keep questioning the way things are, even things that are not usually questioned.

Laci Green says she wants to "get people to talk about sex in a way that isn't shameful, awkward or weird." LACI GREEN

Laci also tries to highlight how important it is to engage in respectful conversations with others, especially when it comes to feminism. It's easy to dismiss someone's point of view or get angry with them if they don't believe the same things you do. In 2017 Laci started a new series of YouTube videos that are respectful conversations with people who hold opinions on feminism different from her own. From this she was able to create productive conversations on important issues and show how to engage in dialogue without shutting others down.

"Feminism is the radical notion that women are human beings."

—*Cheris Kramarae*

Reading someone else's words can be a great way to spark a conversation in real life. My friend Cindy Escobar and I have both read Gloria Steinem's newest book.
ERINNE PAISLEY

"To all the little girls watching...never doubt that you are valuable and powerful and deserving of every chance and opportunity in the world."

—*Hillary Clinton*

5

SMASHING THE GLASS CEILING

DESPITE ALL THE PROGRESS WOMEN HAVE MADE in the last hundred years, they are still extremely underrepresented in many careers. They are also paid less than men for equal work. In Canada, women are usually paid 87 cents for doing a job for which a man would be paid a full dollar. In the United States, the gender wage gap is even wider. One of the major reasons for the wage gap is something referred to as "the glass ceiling"—an invisible barrier that stops women and minorities from advancing professionally.

You can see the effect of the glass ceiling when you look at leadership positions in companies, jobs in STEM (science, technology, engineering and math) and positions in politics. In the most recent Fortune 500 list of top CEOs, women account for only 5.4 percent. Only 11 percent of engineers worldwide are female. Women make up only 22 percent of people working in national politics worldwide. Why? In high school, girls dreamed of having all types of jobs, including CEO, engineer or politician. Now that I'm in university, lots of young women are interested in taking on leadership roles, studying science and getting into politics. Why does their enthusiasm and education not translate into actual jobs?

IN MANY PLACES AROUND THE WORLD, WOMEN HAVE SIGNIFICANTLY FEWER OPPORTUNITIES TO RECEIVE AN EDUCATION.

There are many reasons the glass ceiling exists. As we learned in Chapter 1, in many places around the world, women have significantly fewer opportunities to receive an education.

@chalk.4.change.mhd is an Instagram account run by a group of friends in middle school that gets people to write out facts about girls' education in chalk. These messages are then read by people passing by, which helps spread the word. You can join in with the hashtag #Chalk4Change. **ERINNE PAISLEY**

EVEN THOUGH THERE HAS BEEN SOME PROGRESS, BIASES AND STEREOTYPES ABOUT WOMEN'S ROLES STILL EXIST.

Even though there has been some progress, biases and stereotypes about women's roles still exist. Many people still believe that some work—like engineering—is more appropriate for men. Others think that women should stay home to take care of their children even if they want to be working. Workplaces often don't give enough support—financial and social—to women when they choose to have children, which can cause women to fall behind in workplace environments or not come back to the same position.

Fortunately, many people are working hard every day to make sure the glass ceiling will not exist in the future! For instance, lots of women are excelling in careers that might not have been open to them in the past. Others are fostering inclusive

Girls Who Code

In the United States a program called Girls Who Code aims to "close the gender gap in technology." Girls Who Code was started in New York City in 2012 by lawyer and politician Reshma Saujani to encourage women to consider computer engineering as a career. Girls Who Code programs teach the basics of coding and connect participants to a network of like-minded girls who have a passion for tech. Now there are over fifty thousand graduates of Girls Who Code in the United States. You can learn more about them at their website girlswhocode.com and even start your own chapter in your school or attend their Summer Immersion Programs for free!

FORTUNATELY, MANY PEOPLE ARE WORKING HARD EVERY DAY TO MAKE SURE THE GLASS CEILING WILL NOT EXIST IN THE FUTURE!

Anyone in the United States can apply to participate in the Girls Who Code programs.
GIRLSWHOCODE.COM

Koding with Karlie

Karlie Kloss is a supermodel who loves to code. Karlie says she was always interested in math and science and recently learned how to write code. "Code is a superpower every young woman should be able to access...code is the underlying framework of tech." Karlie started "Kode with Karlie," a summer camp where girls can learn how to code. You must apply for a scholarship to attend. If you get in, you can connect with other girls who are interested in coding—and shattering the glass ceiling! Even if you can't attend one of the summer camps, you can access the online community through the kodewithklossy.com website or @kodewithklossy.

and diverse work environments. Still others are working in media to show women in successful roles, and many more are developing programs to support educational opportunities for women.

According to the United Nations, when more women are working, countries are better off financially. This is called an "economic increase" and is a positive thing for any country. And that's only one of the benefits. Anyone, even you, can help to smash the glass ceiling and make sure women are paid equally and have equal opportunities. Dream big about what type of career you'd like to have and what type of difference you want to make in the world. Support women who are working hard to pursue their dreams by following them on social media. There are programs you can join, such as Girls Who Code, which aims to close the gender gap in technology. You can even contact women who

ACCORDING TO THE UNITED NATIONS, WHEN MORE WOMEN ARE WORKING, COUNTRIES ARE BETTER OFF FINANCIALLY.

are breaking the glass ceiling for advice on how to pursue a similar career—you never know what you'll learn!

STEM

STEM stands for science, technology, engineering and mathematics. These subjects involve asking a lot of questions, learning new ways to create things and problem solving. You might build robots, break apart cells or become an astronaut. Dr. Ellen Stofan was the chief scientist at NASA. Alexa Canady, MD, was the first black woman to become a neurosurgeon. Marie Curie contributed to science through physics and is the first person and only woman to have won two Nobel Prizes. All of these women studied and worked in STEM! In the United States, over 74 percent of high school girls are interested in jobs in these areas. But women make up only 24 percent of people actually working in STEM.

So why do so many girls end up not going into STEM if they are interested? One of the major reasons is because of cultural expectations.

Lots of friendships have started through exploring new passions, and these girls, at an engineering camp in Texas, are meeting new people while learning hands-on skills.
MICHAEL BARERA/WIKIPEDIA.ORG

"How do we change our judgments into curiosity about people? Don't jump to conclusions. Have a little more curiosity."

—Isis Anchalee

Women engineers around the world shared their photos online after Isis Anchalee started #ILookLikeAnEngineer. STEVE JENNINGS/WIKIPEDIA.ORG

STEM jobs have always been male dominated, and many people think it should stay that way. In 2015 Isis Anchalee posed for a poster created by her tech company. Online commenters started questioning if she was a real engineer because she was young, attractive and female. Isis responded by saying, "The negative opinions about this ad that strangers feel so compelled to share illustrate solid examples of the sexism that plagues tech." She started the hashtag #ILookLikeAnEngineer to show that you don't have to be male or look a certain way to be an engineer. The hashtag went viral, and women all over the world started joining in by tweeting photos of themselves with the hashtag to show that anyone who is an engineer looks like an engineer.

#GIRLBOSS

When I was in middle school a lot of people called me "bossy." I liked to lead group projects, be involved in school activities and even make speeches at assemblies. The label started to bother me, and I began to question if I should continue doing the

"BOSSY ISN'T A BAD WORD; IT MEANS YOU HAVE LEADERSHIP POTENTIAL."

things I loved. Was I acting in a way I shouldn't? Was it not acceptable for me to lead projects or make speeches? Hurtful labels and biases, even in middle school, contribute to creating the glass ceiling.

One of my teachers noticed that I was upset and decided to talk to me about it. I still remember exactly what she said, because it changed my decisions about what to be involved in and how to act. She said, "Bossy isn't a bad word; it means you have leadership potential." That one conversation made me think about the word *bossy* in a completely different way. I noticed that it was typically used only to describe women and that it was used to put down outspoken girls who took on leadership roles. I decided not to let a two-syllable word change the way I behaved.

I am definitely not the only one who has been called bossy. Sophia Amoruso worked to reclaim this

Sophia Amoruso is the ultimate #girlboss. At just twenty-three years old she started her first successful business, and even after bankruptcy she has continued to create new projects and make a difference.

KATHY HUTCHINS/SHUTTERSTOCK.COM

word when she wrote her bestselling book *#Girlboss*. Sophia started her own company, Nasty Gal, and talks about how being a #girlboss means being a "boss of your own life." Now there is a #girlboss podcast, a blog and even a television show! The Girlboss Foundation gives funding to projects that are started by women. On Twitter, people have used the hashtags #girlboss and #girlbossmoment to describe times when they have been a boss of their own life. Now moments that might have been described as "bossy" can be celebrated as a #girlbossmoment.

EQUAL VOICES

Politics is another area in which there are significantly fewer women than men. In democracies such as Canada and the United States, politicians are elected to represent the people and address their needs. In Canada, as of 2017, there are 92 female and 246 male members of Parliament. Women hold 104 of 535 seats in the United States Congress. And only about 18 percent of Canadian and American mayors are female.

POP QUIZ

Have you ever had a #girlbossmoment?

You can share your moment on Twitter and join the Girlboss Movement. You can also look up the #girlboss hashtag to see other women's adventures.

How can this be an accurate representation of the populations of these two countries? How can we get more women elected?

Equal Voice is a Canadian organization that works to get more women elected into Canada's Parliament. They accomplish this by raising awareness about women's involvement in politics, trying to change policies, celebrating women in politics and much more. In 2017 they even worked to bring one young woman from each federal riding to the House of Commons in Ottawa, Ontario, for International Women's Day. This project was called Daughters of the Vote, and I was lucky enough to be one of the DOV delegates.

In March 2017, I traveled to Ottawa as the representative for Esquimalt-Saanich-Sooke and sat in the House of Commons to show that a woman's place can be wherever she decides it should be! In Ottawa I met 337 other young women from across Canada who have a commitment to equality. Everyone had a different cause they wanted to share with the world by sitting in Parliament. Some made speeches that were broadcast across Canada about topics such as mental health, transgender rights,

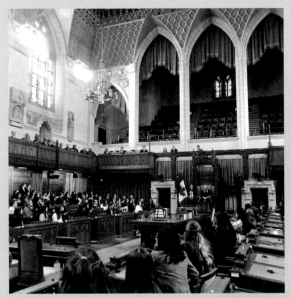

Clockwise from top left: Hearing from Prime Minister Trudeau; making new friends with fellow student representatives; learning from the Honourable Carolyn Bennett, who is the Minister of Crown-Indigenous Relations and Northern Affairs; taking part in leadership workshops; celebrating the first time ever that a trans woman has spoken in the House of Commons; sitting in the Equimalt-Saanich-Sooke designated seat; sharing the hashtag #ElectMoreWomen. **ERINNE PAISLEY**

WOMEN CAN DO ANYTHING THEY PUT THEIR MINDS TO!

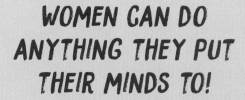

educational funding and Indigenous rights. It was so inspirational to see so many women sitting in the House of Commons, including the largest number of Indigenous representatives ever to assemble in the House and the first transgender person. The event was all over social media and sent a message that was loud and clear: women can do anything they put their minds to!

KEEP ASKING QUESTIONS

Everyone should have equal opportunities to do whatever job they dream of doing—and get paid equally for it too! We have made lots of progress in creating equality when it comes to how our world is run, but there's still so far to go. You can help create a more equal future for everyone, including women and minorities, by questioning what society tells us is "normal." You can support others and show the world that your place is wherever you say it is by working hard and being inclusive.

POP QUIZ

Who are your elected officials?

You can look up online who has been elected to represent your needs and opinions in your town, your province, your state or your country. And you can contact your representatives via email, Facebook or Twitter and tell them about issues that matter to you. Encourage them to take action on topics you think are important. When you can vote, look at what progress has been made and cast your vote wisely. Every ballot has an impact!

POP QUIZ

How can you start a conversation about feminism in your school?

Connect with a leadership group in your school, or with a teacher that you trust, and ask if your school has a budget to fund pizza for an activist discussion event. Invite people in your school to come and eat free pizza and talk about what feminism means to them. It's always good to start off discussion events with a guest speaker. Ask your teachers or parents if they know anyone who could come in and talk about what feminism means to them. Make sure you prepare a few questions beforehand to ask the group, and rehearse what will happen if debates get heated or if people are too shy to share at first.

Kabul Designs

A definite #girlbossmoment occurred when Young Women for Change held a fashion show in Kabul, Afghanistan, and all of the designs were created by women. The event helped to start a conversation in the women's community about how women are seen. The women, who are a part of Young Women for Change, united as one strong voice to challenge what is seen as the "normal" way for women to look and behave. They also were able to show that women can be successful fashion designers and do any job they dream of!

6

POWER PROJECTS

NUMEROUS PROJECTS, ORGANIZATIONS and campaigns are already empowering people all over the world. Many of them have social media accounts that you can follow to get inspired. You can also fundraise and donate money to them to allow them to create even more change. As well, you can even volunteer for some organizations and learn firsthand how you can help empower yourself and those around you.

GIRLS NOT BRIDES

Every single year fifteen million girls around the world are forced to get married before they turn eighteen. This is called *child marriage*. Child marriage happens for many different reasons, including poverty, lack of education and traditional cultural practices. In general, child marriage is able to happen because in some cultures women are seen as having less value than men and are considered a financial burden to their families.

Child marriage is a human rights violation. The Universal Declaration of Human Rights, which was created by the United Nations, says that marriage is only allowed when both people have consented and want to be married to each other. Child marriages often lead to even more human rights violations, including domestic violence and the end of a girl's school education. Child marriage happens all over the world, even in Canada and the United States.

Girls Not Brides is an organization that fights to end this. They bring awareness to the issue so that people know what's happening, learn more about

POP QUIZ

Do you think others in your class know about child marriage?

If not, you can talk to your teacher about doing a project on child marriage and present information about this to the class. On the Girls Not Brides website there is lots of information on child marriage, as well as ways to help stop it. You can even organize a class fundraiser for Girls Not Brides members if you want to do something to help as a class.

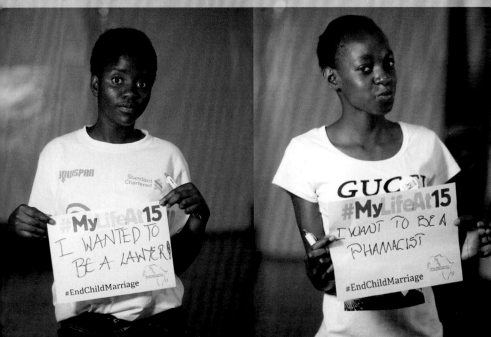

#ENDCHILDMARRIAGE #ENDCHILDMARRIAGE #ENDCHILD

#MyLifeAt15
I want to be
a doctor
#EndChildMarriage

#MyLifeAt15
I wanted
to be a
journalist
#EndChildMarriage

RRIAGE #ENDCHILDMARRIAGE #ENDCHILDMARR

#MyLifeAt15
I wanted to
be a computer
wizard
#EndChildMarriage

#MyLifeAt15
I wanted to
be a
lawyer
#EndChildMarriage

Girls as young as fifteen are often forced to become brides.
These girls shared what their hopes and dreams are at fifteen.
If we work to #EndChildMarriage, their dreams may come true.
GIRLSNOTBRIDES.ORG

the organization and join the fight to end child marriage! They work to make sure laws are enacted to make child marriage illegal. They also work with other organizations to help those who are already affected by child marriage.

HOLLABACK!

In 2014 the YouTube video *10 Hours of Walking in NYC as a Woman* went viral. Over forty-four million people have viewed the video. For ten hours one woman walked through New York while being filmed by a hidden camera. The video shows how much street harassment she experienced. Street harassment is when someone makes unwanted comments, gestures or actions to a stranger in a public space. This could be walking down the street, in a grocery store, in school hallways or on social media. Street harassment happens most frequently to women, LGBTQ+ people and other marginalized groups.

Street harassment not only makes the targets uncomfortable—it is also a threat to their safety. I remember the first time I experienced street harassment. I had just started high school, and a group of men (who looked many years older than me) shouted at my friend and me from a moving car. "Where are you going, pretty ladies?" they yelled. Then they whistled at us. This unwanted attention was not a compliment, and we had not been asking for it. It made us feel unsafe and uncomfortable. Worst of all, we felt powerless because there was nothing we could do to stop it from happening.

WORST OF ALL, WE FELT POWERLESS BECAUSE THERE WAS NOTHING WE COULD DO TO STOP IT FROM HAPPENING.

The New York viral video showed over one hundred instances of street harassment, all directed at one woman over the course of ten hours. The woman was followed by some harassers and shouted at by others. At the end of the video there's information about Hollaback!, a nonprofit organization that fights for gender justice and works to build "safe, inclusive spaces by transforming culture that perpetuates discrimination and violence."

Hollaback! teaches communities what street harassment is through workshops and online resources, and it teaches others how to prevent this from happening. If you have experienced street or online harassment, you can go to ihollaback.org to access resources so you can feel safe and join the movement to end street harassment.

SHE'S THE FIRST

In the summer of 2017 I lived in New York City and interned for a *nongovernmental agency* (NGO) called She's the First (STF), where I learned the most powerful tool you can possess is an education. STF's mission is to fight poverty and gender inequality by providing scholarships to girls around the world who will be the first in their families to graduate high school. There are thirty-one million girls around the world who are the right age to be in primary school but are not attending. Another thirty-four million girls who are the right age to be in higher grades are missing out on their right to receive an education. STF also runs Campus

Clockwise from top left: With my fellow summer interns on #nationalinternday; She's the First's motto; working at the She's the First annual summit in New York City. **ERINNE PAISLEY**

She's the *first*

FIGHT GENDER INEQUALITY THROUGH EDUCATION.

We support girls who will be first in their families to graduate high school and we train students everywhere to be global citizens.

EDUCATION IS A HUMAN RIGHT

Chapters in schools, where students raise money and awareness for women's education by selling STF rainbow cupcakes, organizing conferences to create new conversations and being campus ambassadors for gender equality. In this way STF has started a *social movement* that aims to create global citizens who understand and care about gender equality. If you're in high school or university you can start your own She's the First Campus Chapter by visiting shesthefirst.org. Education is a human right, and Tammy Tibbetts and Christen Brandt, who started She's the First together, believe social media can be used to get more people involved in helping advance these rights. You can also follow them @shesthefirst.

She's the First scholarships provide the opportunity for girls to be able to learn and grow and create a better world together. These scholarships focus on not just getting more girls into school, but also helping them to graduate. There are many factors that can prevent girls from staying in school.

For instance, often when girls get their periods they are forced to drop out of school. If girls do not have access to anything that can catch their menstrual flow, they miss up to two weeks of school a month because they have no option other than bleeding in public. Missed school can then cause them to fall behind in class, and if they fall too far behind to catch up, eventually they will be forced to drop out. These students are the power behind this movement toward gender equality because they fight each and every day to receive their education and create a better world for all those around them!

During the summer of 2017, She's the First launched its newest project: the STF Action Network. This network includes monthly learning modules that anyone can access to learn more about issues that matter. Each month a different topic is covered

THESE STUDENTS ARE THE POWER BEHIND THIS MOVEMENT TOWARD GENDER EQUALITY BECAUSE THEY FIGHT EACH AND EVERY DAY TO RECEIVE THEIR EDUCATION.

using YouTube videos, text and social media posts, which sometimes can seem complicated. The first month was dedicated to Intersectional Feminism. You can sign up to get notifications from the Action Network at action.shesthefirst.org.

WORKING TOGETHER FOR CHANGE

There are many organizations working to create a more equal future and start conversations on what this might look like. If we work together, we can grow from our shared experience. There are lots of ways you can fundraise and bring awareness to these organizations. Often there are examples on their websites or social media of ways to support their projects.

Some ways that I have worked to support other people's projects in the past include baking and selling cupcakes at my school, holding a carwash in my community, organizing a fundraiser concert and even shaving my head for charity! It's fun to work with others to raise money or awareness, and I've made some amazing friends along the way who share the same interests and values as me.

POP QUIZ

What issue matters most to you?

There are many issues that you can fundraise for or bring awareness to, but sometimes it's hard to know which issues to focus on. One way to decide is to find something that means a lot to you personally. Maybe you feel passionate about everyone getting the opportunity to learn in a classroom because you have been able to. Or maybe you want to support LGBTQ+ youth who have been discriminated against because you have gone through a similar experience. The more passion you have for a project, the more others will feel like they want to help too!

"The future depends entirely on what each of us does every day; a movement is only people moving."

—*Gloria Steinem*

7

CONVERSATIONS
IN ACTION

TOPICS LIKE FEMINISM CAN BE DIFFICULT to talk about. It can be confusing to understand fully, and many people get very worked up or defensive when it's brought up. The best way to figure out how to start productive and respectful conversations about gender equality is to learn from others. Fortunately, there are many amazing people out there who have started meaningful conversations about equality.

I'm going to share with you some of my favorite people who have inspired me through the conversations they have started. Sometimes I've learned with them over social media, sometimes through songs and visual art, and sometimes through books or documentaries. You may not have heard of some of these people before, because they come from an older generation, but that doesn't mean that what they have to say isn't innovative and important. In fact, it's often important to learn from the past so that we can start even more powerful conversations in the future and avoid making the same historical mistakes.

BUFFY SAINTE-MARIE

Buffy Sainte-Marie is from the Piapot Cree First Nation in Saskatchewan. She is an artist, musician, public speaker, *philanthropist* and activist. Buffy uses her songs to educate people on the historical mistreatment of Indigenous people in both Canada and the United States.

Indigenous people were already here when the first Europeans arrived, but their rich history has rarely been talked about and taught—until recently. When Europeans came, they massacred the Indigenous people, stole their land and denied them basic human rights. Many Indigenous children were separated from their families and forced to go to residential (or "boarding") schools, where they were often abused. Some never saw their families again. The last residential school in Canada closed in 1996—only one year before I was born.

Schools in Canada and the United States did not teach this part of history for a very long time, and even today they may choose not to. It's hard to admit that our colonial ancestors committed these horrible acts. Buffy believes that in order for everyone to be treated equally in the future, we have to learn about this history and have conversations about it, even if it is painful. Buffy writes songs about this hidden history, and in interviews she always uses some of the time to talk about it. In her song "My Country 'Tis of Thy People You're Dying," she talks about residential schools when she says, *You force us to send our toddlers away/ To your schools where they're taught to despise their traditions.*

Buffy shattered the glass ceiling by creating her own career as an Indigenous international activist and musician. Now almost eighty, she continues to fight for equality and peace through her song lyrics and speeches. She has lectured at schools all over the world about the oppression of Indigenous people and the importance of equality for women. Buffy has shown me how to be a powerful woman and start a conversation through a piece of creative work.

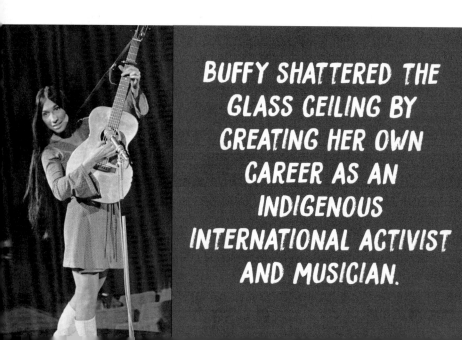

BUFFY SHATTERED THE GLASS CEILING BY CREATING HER OWN CAREER AS AN INDIGENOUS INTERNATIONAL ACTIVIST AND MUSICIAN.

Buffy Sainte-Marie is now seventy-seven years old and continues to create music and make a difference.
DRPETERSTOCKDALE/WIKIPEDIA.ORG

POP QUIZ

Who do you consider a superhero?

What makes a superhero?

A superhero is someone who helps others and is powerful. I consider Buffy Sainte-Marie a superhero. Eight-year-old Michele Threefoot, from Baltimore, Maryland, considers Ruth Bader Ginsburg a superhero. Michele's school had a Superhero Day, and she decided to dress up as this American Supreme Court judge. Judge Ginsburg has spent her whole life fighting for justice and equality. Next Halloween or Superhero Day, think about who you consider to be a superhero. Is there a way you can dress up as your hero? There are more real-life superheroes out there than you might think.

AMANDLA STENBERG'S SOCIAL MEDIA

Amandla is an eighteen-year-old actress, filmmaker and activist who created a YouTube video in 2015 called *Don't Cash Crop My Cornrows*. In it she talks about the history and value of black hairstyles such as cornrows, and then she discusses cultural appropriation. *Cultural appropriation* is the adoption or use of aspects of one culture by members of another culture, without respect and often for profit. Amandla has explained cultural appropriation further by saying, "Appropriation occurs when a style leads to racist generalizations or stereotypes where it originated but is deemed as high-fashion, cool or funny when the privileged take it for themselves."

Through her YouTube video, Amandla started a conversation about cultural appropriation. During this time she also starred in *The Hunger Games* movies as Rue. She gained more and more followers on her social media, especially Instagram. She began using her Instagram to create messages about self-acceptance and love. *When we grow up*

"Appropriation occurs when a style leads to racist generalizations or stereotypes where it originated but is deemed as high-fashion, cool or funny when the privileged take it for themselves."

—Amandla Stenberg

Amandla Stenberg, whose acting career is just taking off, continues to use her growing following on social media to talk about issues that matter to her. OVIDIU HRUBARU /SHUTTERSTOCK.COM

as black girls, we are told that we should be ashamed of our hair. We are told that we should be ashamed of our bodies. And we should be ashamed of our voices. Amandla fights against this by showing images of her natural hair and body in ways that make her feel happy and powerful. This is a great example of intersectional feminism in action!

BEING JAZZ

Even when she was a little kid, Jazz Jennings knew she was a girl trapped in a boy's body. She told her parents that she knew she was a girl even though she had been designated a boy at birth. After a while her parents realized this was not just a phase—it was who Jazz was. They supported her as she transitioned. As I write this, Jazz is sixteen years old and will soon undergo surgery to make her body conform more closely to her gender. Being born one gender but identifying as another is called being *transgender.*

Transgender people meet with a lot of discrimination and lack of acceptance. Jazz decided to start a conversation about being transgender, so she created a YouTube channel called *I Am Jazz* and began to speak out about LGBTQ+ issues every day. Eventually she got a deal to have a television show made about her life as well. And now Jazz has written an autobiography called *Being Jazz*.

Jazz has identified as a feminist in the past and talked about what she sees as the future of feminism. She believes feminism needs to focus on equality and inclusion for all—including transgender people. You can follow Jazz's adventures through her Instagram (where she has nearly half a million followers!) and her YouTube channel.

Jazz Jennings showing off her Pride colours at the NYC Pride Parade in 2016.
STEVEN PISANO/WIKIPEDIA.ORG

POP QUIZ

What is your story?

Each of these activists started conversations about what feminism means to them. They asked people to listen to their stories and invited them to pose questions, give their opinions and engage in conversation. Their stories are meaningful because they are genuine and passionate. It's important to take the time to think about what matters to you. What is your story? What do you truly care about and why? And what can you share with the world that will start a conversation about how to improve it?

GLORIA STEINEM

Like many other people, I have learned a lot from Gloria Steinem, one of the most famous feminists in North America. She is a journalist and social/political activist. Not only does Gloria teach through her words and start conversations with what she says, but she also takes further action. She was at the forefront of feminist protests in the 1960s and continues to be on the front line of the feminist movement.

In 1972 she co-founded *Ms.* magazine, where she was an editor for fifteen years. She continues to serve as a consulting editor. Before *Ms.* magazine, not many women were able to work in media. If they did, they weren't allowed to write about "serious topics"

BEFORE MS. MAGAZINE, NOT MANY WOMEN WERE ABLE TO WORK IN MEDIA. IF THEY DID, THEY WEREN'T ALLOWED TO WRITE ABOUT "SERIOUS TOPICS" SUCH AS POLITICS.

such as politics. Their assignments were mostly about fashion and food and child-rearing—things that women were supposed to be interested in. Gloria wanted to change this. She wanted to talk about women's legal and reproductive rights, politics and anything and everything that affected modern women. She started *Ms.* magazine to do just that. The magazine changed the landscape of media and is still going strong to this day.

Gloria has also written a number of bestselling books on feminism and her life's work. She also helped found the Women's Action Alliance and the National Women's Political Caucus, and she co-founded the Women's Media Center and Voters for Choice, to name just a few organizations she has founded and worked with. She has also been at the forefront of many protests for women's rights, physically standing up for what she believes in. Her presence at the Women's March on Washington in January 2017 was monumental because of her history of supporting powerful movements and protests.

What change makers do you follow on social media?

By following activists who inspire you on social media, you can fill your newsfeed with new ways to create conversations on topics that matter. Some of my favorite people on Instagram are @amandlastenberg, @rowanblanchard, @brielarson, @harinef, @sarainfox, @alishaboe and @rupikaur.

8

THE FUTURE OF FEMINISM

WHAT IS THE FUTURE OF FEMINISM? There's an easy answer for that: the future of feminism is you! Change starts with learning. Learning more about ourselves and learning more from each other. There are many people who have taught me lots about what equality means and how to achieve it. Many are people I have never met. For instance, I have learned a lot about feminism from reading Chimamanda Ngozi Adichie's book *We Should All Be Feminists* in which she shares her own story and starts a conversation about how we all are affected by gender inequality. I also learned a lot from Malala Yousafzai's *I Am Malala*. Most recently I've been reading Gloria Steinem's *My Life on the Road*. I also continue to learn a lot from following @femalecollective, @feministabulous aka Liz Plank, and @rowanblanchard on Instagram.

There is always so much more to learn. Having conversations while you are learning and trying to make change is important. By engaging with others you can learn from their experiences, opinions and mistakes. Engaging in meaningful conversations doesn't just mean talking to people who have the same perspective or who share the same opinions as you. It means learning from all different types of perspectives and learning from opinions that might make you feel uncomfortable.

WORKING WITH OTHERS TO CREATE CHANGE IS ALMOST ALWAYS MORE EFFECTIVE THAN WORKING ALONE.

POP QUIZ

How can you learn something from an opinion that is opposite to your own?

It's easy to shut down other people if they don't agree with you. Try to think about where this person is coming from. Where have they learned these ideas? Where have you learned yours? Can you find some common ground to stand on and then build a productive conversation from there?

The summer interns from She's the First as well as DoSomething.org pose with the digital editor of *Teen Vogue*, Phillip Picardi. Phillip has helped *Teen Vogue* transform into an online platform that provides a place for young people to express themselves and influence the world in a positive way.

DOSOMETHING.ORG

Top: Images from the NYC #IAmAnImmigrant exhibit, which brought attention to President Trump's discriminatory policies. Below: Protesting discriminatory immigration policies, in Toronto, ON, with my friend Phoebe Rogers.
ERINNE PAISLEY

Conversations can also be used to create action. Working with others to create change is almost always more effective than working alone. When working alone, we risk becoming *polarized*. This means that we cling to our own ideas because we can't easily see what we have in common with others. This can create anger and arguments and reduce positive change.

Taking action beyond social media is just as important as initiating it online. Social media can be used as a tool to organize an event or start a conversation between people, which then moves offline to take it to the next level. Action can be creating a social media campaign that brings awareness to an inequality that you have noticed, and it can also be holding a fundraiser for a charity doing work you believe in. It could be volunteering your time to fight for a cause you feel passionately about.

TAKING ACTION BEYOND SOCIAL MEDIA IS JUST AS IMPORTANT AS INITIATING IT ONLINE.

It could even be attending a street protest with a big group of people.

THE WOMEN'S MARCH ON WASHINGTON

On November 8, 2016, Donald Trump was elected president of the United States. His *rhetoric* and policies did not align at all with feminist beliefs and still do not. For instance, he has openly objectified women, fought against reproductive rights for women and banned transgender people from serving in the military. When he was elected, many people, not just those in the United States, were very concerned about what this meant for women's rights.

In response to this, a group of women came up with an idea that would bring together all genders, ages, races, cultures, political affiliations and backgrounds to show support and fight for women's rights, racial and economic justice, as well as many other issues of equality. They would call the event the Women's March on Washington. The march was scheduled to occur the day after Donald Trump was inaugurated. The event went viral, and people all around the world started to plan their own Women's Marches to show solidarity for women and minority rights.

When the day came, almost five million people across the United States marched in their local Women's Marches. Marches were held in eighty-four different countries, everywhere from Paris, France, to Antarctica. I attended the Women's March in Toronto, Ontario, with four of my close friends. It was amazing to see so many like-minded people come together to show solidarity for rights we all felt were being threatened and start a more positive narrative about why these rights matter. It gave me hope that even when the people in charge do not believe in upholding basic human rights, there are still people out there who will fight alongside you to protect them!

MARCHES WERE HELD IN EIGHTY-FOUR DIFFERENT COUNTRIES, EVERYWHERE FROM PARIS, FRANCE, TO ANTARCTICA.

EVEN WHEN THE PEOPLE IN CHARGE DO NOT BELIEVE IN UPHOLDING BASIC HUMAN RIGHTS, THERE ARE STILL PEOPLE OUT THERE WHO WILL FIGHT ALONGSIDE YOU TO PROTECT THEM!

The Women's March in Toronto, ON, in January 2017 was a truly inspirational event. **ERINNE PAISLEY**

Women of all ages attended the
Women's March in Toronto.
ERINNE PAISLEY

Action is most effective when you are able to speak to something that has real meaning for you. The more an issue matters to you, the more meaningful your action becomes. Once you have identified your cause, choose a way to express yourself. Creativity is key when taking action about issues that matter. Maybe you have a special talent for writing or creating YouTube videos. Maybe you could design a great website. Or maybe you have always loved painting or in-line skating. Any passion can be turned into action when matched with an issue that matters.

For instance, a friend of mine from university writes a column on what it is like to be a female, Muslim university student living in Toronto. Through this she has used creativity to share her experiences and start new conversations. Another friend organized a concert in a local restaurant to raise money for CARE, a nonprofit organization that works to defeat poverty and increase social justice. Someone else I know used his public-speaking skills to host a number of short TV shows for Vice Media, which covers political topics such as *immigration rights*.

Feminism is a topic that can and should be talked about forever and learned about forever. It affects all of us. It's not just about women. It's about the way our world works and the systems that humans have put in place to make the world function the way it does. Hopefully this book will encourage you to look more closely at the world around you, think about the way things can change for the better and, above all, start conversations about the things that matter to you.

And remember to see change, share change and be change.

You can follow PopActivism on Instagram @pop_activism and twitter @popactivism. You can also visit popactivism.com to read new posts and even submit your own!

popactivism

see change. share change. be change

ADDITIONAL PHOTO CREDITS

Page 1 FRANKLIN D ROOSEVELT LIBRARY WEBSITE/WIKIPEDIA.ORG

Page 13 KOSTAS KOUTSAFTIKIS/SHUTTERSTOCK.COM

Page 29 IDOMINICK/WIKIPEDIA.ORG

Page 36 ERINNE PAISLEY

Page 54 UNDERWOOD & UNDERWOOD/WIKIPEDIA.ORG

Page 60 ERINNE PAISLEY

Page 70 STEMOC/WIKIPEDIA.ORG

Page 96 ERINNE PAISLEY

Page 110 LYNN GILBERT/WIKIPEDIA.ORG

Page 114 NATIONAAL ARCHIEF/WIKIPEDIA.ORG

Page 124 LYNN GILBERT, GAGE SKIDMORE, LIBRARY OF CONGRESS/WIKIPEDIA.ORG

Page 126 DOSOMETHING.ORG

Page 139 ERINNE PAISLEY

Page 141 ERINNE PAISLEY

Page 145 ERINNE PAISLEY

GLOSSARY

abortion—the intentional termination of a pregnancy, typically during the first twenty-eight weeks, before the fetus is fully formed

ally—a person who supports the rights and freedoms of a marginalized or oppressed group that he or she is not part of

body shaming—the act of humiliating someone by making mean comments about their body shape, size or general appearance

child marriage—a formal marriage or informal union entered into before the age of eighteen

consensual—agreed upon by all parties, particularly in relation to sex

contraception—methods or techniques used to prevent pregnancy, such as condoms, contraceptive pills, intrauterine devices and male or female sterilization

cultural appropriation—the adoption or use of aspects of one culture by members of another culture, without respect and often for profit

feminism—the advocacy of women's rights based on the belief that men and women are equal

gender bias—unequal treatment and expectations based on a person's sex

glass ceiling—a barrier created by people and/or organizations that prevents women and minorities from advancing professionally

human rights—the rights and freedoms that belong to all people, no matter their nationality, place of residency, sex, ethnic origin, color, religion, language or any other factor

hypermasculinity—exaggerated stereotypical male traits and behavior, such as physical strength, aggression and hyper-sexuality

immigration rights—the legal rights designated to any person who is moving permanently to a country they are not originally from

intersectionality—the interconnectedness of such factors as race, class and gender as they apply to a person's or group's experiences

nongovernmental organization (NGO)—a local, national or international group that does not function to make a profit, is run by citizens and works toward a clear cause

nonconsensual—not agreed upon by one or more people involved

philanthropist—a person who aims to help others by donating money to specific causes

public service announcement (PSA)—a message that informs the public about an important topic or issue and is distributed free of charge

rhetoric—effective or persuasive speaking or writing

sexism—prejudice, stereotyping or discrimination on the basis of a person's sex

social movement—a group of people and/or organizations working toward changing the way society functions

STEM—acronym for science, technology, engineering and mathematics

street harassment—a form of sexual harassment that includes unwanted comments, "wolf whistling," catcalling and other actions by strangers in public areas

suffragist—a woman fighting for the right to vote through organized protest

RESOURCES

ONLINE

CHAPTER 1
malala.org

CHAPTER 2
feministing.com
heforshe.org
teenvogue.com
unwomen.org/en

CHAPTER 3
amysmartgirls.com
facebook.com/feminismonbustle
lennyletter.com
rookiemag.com
womenyoushouldknow.net

CHAPTER 4
plannedparenthood.org
youtube.com/user/lacigreen

CHAPTER 5
equalvoice.ca
girlboss.com
kodewithklossy.com
girlswhocode.com

CHAPTER 6
girlsnotbrides.org
ihollaback.org
shesthefirst.org

CHAPTER 8
chimamanda.com

PRINT

Adichie, Chimamanda Ngozi. *We Should All Be Feminists*.
New York: Anchor Books, 2015.

Armstrong, Sally. *Ascent of Women*.
Toronto: Random House Canada, 2013.

Sandberg, Sheryl. *Lean In: Women, Work, and the Will to Lead*.
New York: Alfred A. Knopf, 2013.

Steinem, Gloria. *My Life on the Road*.
New York: Random House, 2015.

Yousafzai, Malala. *I Am Malala*.
New York: Little, Brown and Company, 2013.

ACKNOWLEDGMENTS

I AM FORTUNATE TO HAVE MANY STRONG and compassionate women in my life who have shown me what it means to use one's creative energy to empower others. I've mentioned many of these women in previous acknowledgments, and the list keeps growing:

My mother, Julia Menard.

My grandmother, Mary Lesiw.

Briana Brown, Suzy Green, Penny Barner and Margie.

To the team at Orca—you have helped create a powerful book series that I could never have fully imagined on my own. Thank you for believing in this project and for taking young people seriously in all your work! Jenn Playford and Sarah Harvey, thank you for working so closely with me on this project and helping me fine-tune my "voice" on the page. Andrew Wooldridge, thank you for believing in this project and taking a chance on an idealistic high school student. And Melissa Shirley, thank you for seeing this project through to the finish line and taking it to places and people who would not have otherwise seen it. Working with you has been an absolute treat.

Thank you to my dad, Brian Paisley, and my brother, Stuart Paisley, for showing me what it means to use your space to empower others and share your voice.

And, finally, I dedicate this book to Erin Hayes and Alana Charlton, women who showed me how to be a fearless and powerful female leader. In elementary school, Erin Hayes took me aside and told me that when someone called me "bossy," it just meant that I had leadership potential. In high school, Alana Charlton embodied someone who is not "bossy" but is a powerful boss. She is relentlessly passionate about her job and about empowering the young people around her.

I hope to be able to pass along the gifts that Erin and Alana gave to me—and hopefully this book is a start.

So to all you "bossy girls" out there...this one's for you.